# Quetzalcoatl: The History and Legacy of the Feath Mesoamerican Mythology

## By Ernesto Novato and Charles River

Quetzalcoatl in the Codex Telleriano-Remensis

# About Charles River Editors

**Charles River Editors** is a boutique digital publishing company, specializing in bringing history back to life with educational and engaging books on a wide range of topics. Keep up to date with our new and free offerings with this 5 second sign up on our weekly mailing list, and visit Our Kindle Author Page to see other recently published Kindle titles.

We make these books for you and always want to know our readers' opinions, so we encourage you to leave reviews and look forward to publishing new and exciting titles each week.

# Introduction

**A depiction of the god**

# Quetzalcoatl

Gilgamesh, Hercules, Aeneas, and Lancelot are instantly recognized as mythological heroes in the West, evoking visions of Persian monsters, ghastly labors, and the founding and glorification of cities, but the name Quetzalcoatl is as mysterious as its spelling. Even those who have come across his name when learning about the history of Mesoamerica – particularly the Aztec and the god's role in the Spanish conquest of their empire – are often unaware that the Mesoamerican deity has tales that equal any of those in the repertoire of the mythological figures mentioned above, and the tale of his transmission into modern times is no less fascinating.

As archaeologists quickly learned, there are numerous temples dedicated to Quetzalcoatl all across Mesoamerica. From the Aztec to the Maya, Quetzalcoatl - the Feathered Serpent - rears his beautiful head from magnificent relief carvings in temples no less grandiose than the largest pyramid in the region, that of Cholula in Mexico. Furthermore, thousands of people still gather in the great Mayan city of Chichén Itzá during the spring and autumn equinoxes to watch the shadow of the Feathered Serpent slither its way down the temple known as El Castillo.

Worship of the Feathered Serpent can be traced back 2,000 years, and the Serpent's cults appear all across Mesoamerica. The Olmec, the Aztec, and both the Yucatec and K'iche Mayans all had different names for this deity, including Kukulkan, Q'uq'umatz, and Tohil, but his iconography is curiously consistent over several centuries across the region. Depending on who was worshipping him, the Feathered Serpent was a creator-god, the god of the winds, the god of the rains, or merely a near-divine ancestor whose militaristic ways won his followers land and riches before he was eventually marred by lavishness and iniquity, resulting in his demise.

To some of the invading Spanish conquistadores, Quetzalcoatl was little more than another demon the "natives" had been worshipping before they were kind enough to bring God to the New World. To others, however, Quetzalcoatl was precisely evidence of the spread of Christianity reaching Mesoamerica long before the conquistadores ever arrived. Much of what modern scholars depend on to understand Quetzalcoatl, however, comes from the period of the Spanish invasion of Mesoamerica, and therefore stories of his blowing the sun across the sky have become mixed with those linking him with Jesus Christ. Nevertheless, this makes for a fascinating picture of a deity whose image has been shaped by some of the most famous civilizations in history and continues to be adopted by people today, often for more than spiritual purposes (as is evident in the adoption of Quetzalcoatl imagery in Mexico's struggle for independence). As a result, Quetzalcoatl was and remains one of the most interesting and enlightening stories ever to have come out of any civilization, and his stories offer a better understanding of the Mesoamerican world.

*Quetzalcoatl: The History and Legacy of the Feathered Serpent God in Mesoamerican Mythology* examines the origins of the deity and his place in the pantheon of gods. Along with pictures of important people, places, and events, you will learn about Quetzalcoatl like never before.

Quetzalcoatl: The History and Legacy of the Feathered Serpent God in Mesoamerican Mythology

## The Olmec and the Feathered Serpent

Historians believe people have lived in Mesoamerica for around 25,000-40,000 years, ever since they most likely strode across the ice bridge on the Bering Strait. Hunter-gatherer groups abandoned their nomadic ways with the advent of agriculture and many small communities began dotting the mountains and valleys of Mesoamerica henceforth.

Mesoamerica is the name given to the geographical and cultural area in Central and North America generally encompassing the area from the desert north of the Valley of Mexico across Guatemala and Honduras (including Belize and El Salvador) to western Nicaragua and Costa Rica. It was in this region that a number of societies flourished before the Spanish conquest effectively ended the advancement of Mesoamerican cultures like the Aztec and Inca.

**A map of Mesoamerican sites**

As a cultural area, Mesoamerica is defined by the advent of a number of cultural traits developed and subsequently shared by indigenous populations of the region, beginning around 7000 BCE with the farming of maize/corn, beans, squash, and chilis, as well as the domestication of turkeys and dogs. This subsequently set in motion a transition from migratory Paleoindian hunter-gatherer societies into organized, sedentary agricultural societies. Today, the groups are defined by their agricultural practices, distinct architectural styles, complex mythological and religious traditions, a calendar system, and a tradition of ball-playing.

The cultural evolution that took place in Mesoamerica prior to the arrival of Europeans is considered extraordinary by any measure. With evidence of potterymaking appearing in the fossil record by 2000 BCE, it seems science and technology clearly became motivational factors for the Olmec and subsequent cultures, if only to produce artifacts that were spiritual in significance. Art, for example, quickly evolved from simple referential imagery to symbolic writing, with texts varying in form and complexity based on the time period, the specific culture, and language. No true alphabet was ever developed for these early forms of writing, making decipherment arduous even for modern linguists.

Other art involved not just the graphic (used to express ideological concepts or features of nature) but the monumental, such as the advent of flat-topped pyramids thought by many historians to have spawned the "moundbuilder" traditions in North America, as exemplified by the Adena and Hopewell of Ohio, and the Mississippian of the Mississippi River Valley and U.S. Southeast. Scholars do not know with certainty which cultures conceived and developed various other innovations, but metalworking, astronomy, arithmetic, the calendar, and advanced irrigation techniques are typically attributed to the Mesoamerican people. The overlapping of Maya, Teotihuacáno, Toltec, and Aztec histories makes it nearly impossible to discern who to credit with these and other advances, but given all of these cultural advancements, it stands to reason that one of the most influential civilizations in the region is the oldest.

By all indications, once the settlement process began, within just a few centuries, a major independent culture emerged from the lowlands of Veracruz and Tabasco on the Gulf Coast of Mexico: the Olmec. One of the earliest known complex civilizations of Mesoamerica, the Olmec settled the Gulf Coast of Mexico and then extended its sphere of influence inland and southwards across the Isthmus of Tehuantepec. This period of cultural development also saw the institution of class stratification, an establishment of chiefdoms with large corresponding ceremonial centers, and the organization of a network of interconnected trade routes for dealing cacao, ceramics, cinnabar, hematite, jade, obsidian, and Spondylus shells.

**A map of the region**

If one thing can be said about the development of civilizations out of villages in Mesoamerica, it is that, for all the power held by certain cultural centers, they were all connected to each other by a complex web of trade routes from a very early date. Mesoamerican villages seem to have embraced the iconography and religious practices and they incorporated them into their own cultures successfully until the Spanish conquest and, arguably, continue to do so until this day. Nevertheless, there were hubs of sociopolitical (not to mention militaristic) might across Mesoamerica, the first of which might be said to have been the center of the Olmec culture (ca. 1500-1 BCE).

Around 1200 BCE, considerably large community centers grew up across southern Mexico, and the religions that emerged from them flowed along the trade routes. With every community that adopted them, the views and characters became more solidified in the minds of the believers.

The Olmec left the first images of the celestial Feathered Serpent appear, and yet the existence of the Olmec civilization was only first ascertained through examination of artifacts acquired by antiquity dealers purchased via the pre-Columbian art market in the late 19th and early 20th centuries. While all Olmec artwork is striking in style and execution, as exemplified by exquisite representations of jaguar crafted from jade, it is the giant colossal basalt head statues - some weighing more than 20 tons - that have provided the greatest insight into the Olmec culture. With discovery of the first such giant head in 1862 near the Veracruz district of San Andres Tuxtla, scholars were able to get a clue about the Olmec sphere of influence, because basalt (a type of volcanic rock) is not indigenous to the Gulf Coast region and thus had to have been transported great distances over land and water to accommodate their sculpting needs.

When archaeologists first began excavation of the Olmec heartland, an area now demarcated as lying between the Tuxtla Mountains and the Olmec principal site of La Venta and extending some 50 miles inland from the Gulf of Mexico, they began to discover Olmec artifacts far from the Gulf Coast. Given the distance, they were initially doubtful the ancient inhabitants were actually Olmec, figuring instead that they were finding remains from other Mesoamerican groups who had acquired Olmec objects through trade. Ultimately, the realization that the Olmec had successfully established and maintained far-flung trade to acquire basalt, jade, magnetite, and serpentine ore provided the first significant insight into the workings of Olmec society.

Though far from clearly defined even today, it is apparent that the Olmec religious system influenced all successive Mesoamerican cultures, including the Maya, Zapotec, Teotihuacáno, Toltec, Mixtec, and Aztec, up to and even beyond the arrival of the Spanish in 1519. But their contribution to complex societal development in Mesoamerica and even the whole of Mexico is far more significant. While is has been argued that the Olmec were not the first organized culture in the area, evidence suggests that their settlement at San Lorenzo most likely represents the first major population center. San Lorenzo was the first city to be founded with a ceremonial center/pyramid-mound at its core (a center requiring the moving of millions of cubic tons of earth by the basketload), the first socially-organized, advanced metropolis (with a stratified society segregated into priest, merchant, and craftsmen classes), the first fully-actualized commerce center (where Mesoamerican traders dealt in exotic goods including salt, cocoa beans, bird feathers, jaguar pelts, and grinding stones), and monumental art reflecting hero-gods or perhaps ruler lineage.

While virtually nothing can be stated with certainty about the Olmec's spiritual beliefs, it is generally accepted that Olmec religious activities were performed by a combination of rulers, full-time priests, and perhaps shaman. Since their society was quite stratified, scholars believe that the Olmec rulers were considered the most important religious figures, and that they derived their legitimacy as rulers by associating themselves with Olmec deities.

According to oral tradition, the Olmec belief system (as well as those of subsequent Mesoamerican cultures) reflected a cosmic view in which all elements and creatures were infused with spiritual energy that provided the universe its momentum. Based on cross-cultural studies, particularly those of Native American societies, scholars speculate that the Olmec may have tried to gain access to this spiritual power through different kinds of disciplines and rituals, such as fasting, meditation, and possibly even physical mutilation and blood-letting. Some have gone so far as to assert that the Olmec routinely practiced violent forms of human sacrifice, such as decapitation, and then passed the practice on to other groups like the Maya.

Although their role is not clearly-defined, there is considerable physical evidence that the Olmec had shamans or some other form of holymen, particularly in the so-called transformation figures. Some historians have likened these shaman to astrologers, and there is some evidence that suggests shamans engaged in rituals designed to access animal spirits that could help transcend human consciousness. Olmec shamans may also have prepared special hallucinogens which were inhaled to induce altered states of consciousness, a ritual common to indigenous groups of both upper North America and South America. Olmec sculpture suggests that shaman attempted to assume the jaguar spirit using jade masks carved with a combination of feline and human features. As an animal whose existence combined the elements of land, water, and air through living in the jungle, swimming in rivers, lakes, and streams, and hunting both during the day and night, the jaguar clearly held special respect and spiritual significance. Olmec art and artifacts frequently depict jaguars, and the American eagle may have been perceived as the jaguar of the sky, with one sculpture portraying what has been interpreted as a flying jaguar with a human passenger on his back.

While no oral history about Olmec mythology survives, interpretations of monuments and other artifacts (such as the Las Limas figure at Veracruz), as well as studies of the mythology of subsequent Mesoamerican groups, have combined to offer a possible glimpse into what Olmec mythology may have been like. If accurate, it was a complex system of beliefs that were eventually replaced with legends about living Olmec hero-god rulers. Furthermore, Quetzalcoatl, the Feathered Serpent deity, is well represented in Olmec art, leading researchers to believe that the pantheon of deities found in Maya, Teotihuacáno, Toltec, and Aztec culture can be traced all the way back to the Olmec.

The great bird-serpent/priest-king Quetzalcoatl is often compared to other ancient gods, like Ra for the ancient Egyptians, Enki for the Sumerians, and Nu Kua for the Chinese, but in Olmec culture, the Plumed Serpent was unique because he transformed from myth to god to human and back to myth, seemingly at will. Elusive and intangible, but at the same time permanent, the Olmec believed Quetzalcoatl would be physically incarnated at times, while at other times Quetzalcoatl essentially represented a kind of fairy tale story where anything is possible and things are constantly transforming into something else.

**This Olmec artifact is the earliest known depiction of the serpent deity.**

Conceived some 1500 years before the birth of Christ, Quetzalcoatl not only formed the mythical basis for the Olmec religious worldview but was believed to have materialized as one or more living rulers, after which he went on to be held as a kind of religious messiah by numerous Mesoamerican cultures to follow. According to French anthropologist Claude Levi-Strauss, "all available variants of a myth must be taken into account. There is no single, true version," a perspective that can be aptly applied to the myth of Quetzalcoatl. Indeed, few mythological characters are deemed legends and afforded biographical status as Quetzalcoatl has.

To the Aztec and several Mesoamerican cultures preceding them, history was not a straight linear timeline of events but a series of cycles described by Mexican historian Guillermo Batalla (1935-1991) as "a spinning wheel spiraling forward through time, engendering repetitions as it goes." According to Aztec beliefs, the god who set this wheel in motion was Plumed Serpent Quetzalcoatl, the Lord of the Dawn and Phoenix of the West. He was the namer of all things in the universe, and according to the Florentine Codex (the 16th century ethnographic account of Franciscan friar Bernardino de Sahagún), "He was the wind, he was the guide, the roadsweeper of the rain gods, of the masters of water, of those who brought rain. Legend recounts that Quetzalcoatl gathered together the remains of the human race from Mictlan (the Underworld; the Realm of the Dead) after the primeval flood and then reestablished humanity in the Time Before Time."

As the legend is told, Plumed Serpent took an assemblage of bones, ashes, and clay and infused his own sacred blood to form man, and then blessed him with maize, the arts of weaving and mosaic-making, music and dance, the science of curing illness, crafts, time, the stars in the heaven, the calendar, prayers, and sacrifice. Plumed Serpent was the performer of miracles, the supreme magician, the ruler of sorcerers, holding the secret of all enchantments. But as the legend further explains, Plumed Serpent's plans for humanity were frequently thwarted by his alter ego/dark side Tezcatlipoca, known also as Smoking Mirror, referred to in legend as his evil twin. Setting out to foil his good works, Tezcatlipoca posed as a servant to infiltrate Plumed Servant's holy monastery, then brewed pulque, a concoction derived from the maguey plant, which he served to Tezcatlipoca and his sister—then convinced him to have intercourse with her. Having broken his vows of chastity, Plumed Serpent was cast out of the monastery—scarred by his spiritual transgression. Now fallen from grace, Quetzalcoatl abandoned his earthly possessions and began what would become an epic hero's journey, beginning at Tollan (the future Toltec center).

Gaining fame throughout Mexico for his pilgrimage of purification, from Cholula (near present-day Puebla de Zaragoza in Central Mexico) to Chichen Itza, when Quetzalcoatl reached the shore of the holy sea at Tlillan Tlapallan (the Land of the Black and Red on the Gulf Coast of Mexico), he told his followers that he had been called forth, thus evolving into his messianic form. Directing his followers to build a raft of snakes, he donned a turquoise mask and promised to return in the year Ce Acatl or One Reed, a year that cycled every 52 years according to the calendar. Navigating out to sea, Plumed Serpent suddenly burst into flames, with the ashes of his heart rising upwards into the heavens and becoming the planet Venus. From that time on, he rose in the sky each morning to announce the rebirth of the sun. Perhaps most notably, Ce Acatl corresponded to the year 1519 in the modern European calendar, which also happened to be the year Spanish ships first appeared on the horizon of Veracruz.

Quetzalcoatl was not the only religious innovation on the part of the Olmec, however. They also appear to have expressly instigated the importance of mountains in Mesoamerican religion, expressed explicitly in the form of the many pyramids across the landscape, and the connection between caves and the birth of the human race. These themes would gain more importance in the religious mindset of Mesoamericans long after the eventual fall of the Olmec civilization in the 4th century BCE.

## Monte Albán

In the Valley of Oaxaca, where southern Mexico bends eastwards towards Guatemala, Belize and its own Yucatan peninsula, lies the magnificent settlement of Monte Albán. Despite its location in a valley, Monte Albán is situated atop an easily defensible hill with very little in the way of natural resources (including fresh water) which has prompted some scholars to presume that it was established during a politically turbulent era.[1] Despite the difficulty offered to the inhabitants, the Zapotec people, by their natural surroundings, Monte Albán was a successful cultural center for the better part of half a millennium.

Today, almost 200 tombs, 2000 terraced slopes, a ballcourt, and numerous palaces and pyramid tombs can still be seen at Monte Albán. The pyramids appear to take on a similar symbolic role as they did with the Olmec civilization, used as imitation holy mountains used for ceremonies often involving the dead and the underworld. Here, the artwork is equally accomplished and there are many images of agricultural gods and gods of the rain, including the Feathered Serpent again. These images are found amongst another common symbol associated with Quetzalcoatl: that of the opossum.

Opossums have been prevalent in Mesoamerica for centuries and have always been given similar characteristics to the other trickster deity, the Coyote, in North American stories. The opossums - scavengers and fierce fighters when pushed - appear in much of Zapotec artwork, and one figurine was found in a temple to Quetzalcoatl.[2] The symbolic connection between the opossum and Quetzalcoatl is multifaceted in that they were both thought to be connected to the dawn, the discovery of corn, rain, and even stealing fire. These aspects are important to the character of Quetzalcoatl in no small part for being key, universal aspects of trickster deities.

Quetzalcoatl's imagery at Monte Albán reveals his connection with the opossum, sacred mountains, and Mesoamerican religious thought as a whole, but Monte Albán pales in comparison with its neighbor and occasional master, Teotihuacán.

## The Toltec and *Teotihuacán*

To the north of Monte Albán, just northeast of Mexico City, lie the ruins of Teotihuacán. Teotihuacán is the name the Aztec gave to the city - long beyond its zenith and mostly ruins in their time - which they believed was the "place where the gods were created."[3] They gave the

---

[1] Knight 2012
[2] Read 2000
[3] ibid.

city this name due to its monumental structures, and the myth that grew out of their weather-beaten cracks was that this was the site where the gods created the fifth Sun, the age of humans.

Archaeological evidence has provided a great many clues about the Toltec culture, and the modern-day Pascua Yaqui have contributed considerable oral history to the Mesoamerican picture, but most of what is known today about the Toltec comes from the so-called Aztec Chronicles, oral and written accounts that have faced decades of scrutiny from the world's top Mesoamerican scholars as they attempt to separate genuine history from historic distortions written to glorify Aztec rule. After centuries of being categorized as an Aztec invention for the purpose of claiming a distinguished heritage, historians today identify the Toltec based on three other interrelated cultural groups: the Teotihuacános (who are believed to have thrived as a society for nearly 750 years before the Toltec assumed control of their capital city of Teotihuacán and built Tollán on the ruins); the Aztec (who followed in the Toltec's footsteps and used their cultural model in founding their capital city of Tenochtitlan); and the Pascua Yaqui (a Uto-Azteca people said to have descended from the ancient Toltec and migrated into the United States by the end of 19th century.

According to the archaeological record, about 1 CE, a culture known as the Teotihuacáno emerged just outside modern-day Mexico City and began constructing a massive capital city that at its peak may have sustained a population of more than 200,000. Laid out in what would still be considered a modern design, Teotihuacán had wide streets, numerous town squares, markets, and plazas, well over 2,000 apartment buildings, and perhaps most significantly, over 600 pyramids believed to have been used for religious purposes. Though various districts of the city appear to have provided housing for influential individuals from across the Teotihuacáno sphere of influence, scholars note the absence of fortifications and military installations, which suggests they had a peaceful co-existence with their neighbors. Believed to have reached its pinnacle by 450 A.D., this massive city, which covered nearly 12 square miles, seems to have represented a culture of unprecedented power whose sphere of influence extended some 10,000 square miles across much of Mesoamerica, as far south as Guatemala.

Widely known as a center of industry and trade, Teotihuacán maintained a large artistic sector that was full of potters, jewelers, and craftsmen recognized for exquisite obsidian goods. But after thriving for perhaps 650 years, the city faced a drastic decline, with invaders from the north conquering and burning down the palaces, temples, and places used by the upper classes. Scholars still debate whether the invaders were the Toltec themselves or whether the Toltec simply rose to prominence by waiting for Teotihuacán to disintegrate.

**The ruins of Teotihuacán**

While modern scholars debate the extent and degree of Teotihuacano influence - with some believing they maintained militaristic dominance and others believing that adoption of foreign traits was part of their cultural modus operandi - there seems little doubt that the city of Teotihuacán had a major influence on the Late Preclassic and Classic Maya (400 BCE-100CE and 250-900 CE, respectively). This may have been accomplished by the conquest of a number of Maya centers, including Tikal and the region of Peten, as hieroglyphic inscriptions made by the Maya describe their encounters with Teotihuacano conquerors. It's also widely believed that the Teotihuacano influenced the Toltec, and thus the Aztec and Yaqui cultures indirectly, regardless of whether the Toltec conquered the Teotihuacano or not.

According to Aztec oral and written history, the Mexica (the Aztec protogroup) originated in Aztlán, a place generally assumed to have been located somewhere north of the Valley of Mexico. However, many historians think the Mexica may have originated as far north as the U.S. Southwest. The Mexica were a Nahuatl-speaking group thought to have included the Chichimeca peoples, who were actually many different groups with varying ethnic and linguistic affiliations that adopted the Aztec designation after the founding of Tenochtitlan and the Aztec empire. Based on Aztec codices and other regional histories, the Mexica arrived at Chapultepec (in modern-day Mexico City) around 1248 A.D., and at that time, Chapultepec was formerly a

Teotihuacano settlement and currently a Toltec one.

At the time of their arrival, the Valley of Mexico had many city-states competing for resources, the most powerful of which was the Culhuacan culture to the south and the Azcapotzalco culture to the west. After the Mexica were expelled from Azcapotzalco, presumably for their barbaric habits, in 1299, the Culhuacan ruler Cocoxtli gave the Mexica permission to settle in the barren reaches of Tizapan, where they are thought to have assimilated Culhuacan culture. According to legend, in 1323 the Mexica were directed by a vision to a small swampy island in Lake Texcoco, where by 1325 they founded Tenochtitlan as the heart of what became the Aztec empire.

At first, Tenochtitlan was officially a satellite of Azcapotzalco, which at the time was a regional power. But during a regional power play, the so-called Triple Alliance was formed by the rulers of Tenochtitlan, Texcoco, and Tlacopan, who proceeded to defeat Azcapotzalco in 1428. For the next century, the Alliance dominated the Valley of Mexico, slowly extending its power base to the Gulf of Mexico and west to the Pacific Ocean. During this time, Tenochtitlan gradually became the dominant power within the alliance, and thus the Aztec became the dominant civilization. Though still officially part of the Triple Alliance, the Aztec systematically imposed their political hegemony far beyond the Valley of Mexico, supplanting local customs with their complex mythological, religious, architectural and artistic traditions and effectively establishing themselves as imperial rulers. During their rise to power, the Aztec would claim descent from the Toltec, and in some cases, they claimed to have defeated the Toltec in early battles. The Aztec claimed to have usurped the Toltec's social and religious institutions (including their gods), incorporated sacred Toltec lands into their own, and promoted what are now widely believed to be exaggerated or even fabricated accounts of Toltec accomplishments to bolster their own cultural standing in the region.

The most fascinating aspect of Teotihuacán is that its monumental structures formed a city whose entire structure mirrored that of the Mesoamerican cosmos. It is oriented 15°25' east of north so that it aligned with both the Pleiades and the movement of the sun.[4] The main "street" - later called "Avenue of the Dead" - runs north-south and is cross-sectioned by a river the people of Teotihuacán diverted in order to divide their city into four quadrants. This is a key symbol - that of a four-petaled Flower - which will be discussed further below.

At the northern end of the "Avenue of the Dead" is situated the Pyramid of the Moon, which looks like a miniature version of the mountain that stands behind it. Halfway down the "Avenue" lies the Pyramid of the Sun on the eastern side, beneath the very center of which archaeologists have discovered a very significant cave that once had a spring. This cave was also hewn into the shape of a four-petaled flower. In the southern sector lies the structure known as the "Ciudadela" and, within it at the heart of the city, a smaller temple with imagery of the Feathered Serpent all around it.

---

[4] ibid.

It is on this "Ciudadela" where the most elaborate depictions of the Feathered Serpent appear. A giant head protrudes from the walls with a Cheshire grin made of imposing predatory teeth. Attached to the head is a body which appears to flow though water alongside shells and other marine animals. This is important because, in later years, Quetzalcoatl came to be associated with the wind and the rain.

There is another head on this temple, however, that continues to baffle modern scholars today. It does not have much of the familiar symbolism associated with any of the other gods of the time but one theory is that this head with a kind of "flaming headdress" could represent the "dry season" in comparison with the Feathered Serpent's "wet season." Although representing a wet season through the use of marine animals and water-like depictions in art is considerably easier than depicting the dry season, scholars have surmised that the "fiery" headdress represents war, and that the time of year for war was the "dry season," not the "wet."[5] Supporting this theory is the evidence of an extremely large burial site of war captives inside this temple.

Mountains, caves, four-petaled flowers, and water are all key to understanding how Mesoamerican people constructed their cosmos in both tangible and intangible ways. When the Aztec discovered the ruins of Teotihuacán, they were in awe at the size of the structures, but their symbolic meaning was obviously not lost on them either. The Aztec put great emphasis on the growth of maize, and therefore it is unsurprising that they also considered water sources to be centers of great importance as well. Archaeologists discovered evidence of child sacrifice in the cave - again, associated with the birth of humankind, just like at Monte Albán - which was also a practice under the Aztec in which children were sacrificed to important water sources. At the Temple of the Feathered Serpent, there is more evidence of human sacrifice and numerous images presumably connecting these warriors' blood with life-giving water.

As ghastly and gruesome as the idea of human sacrifice is to people today, it's important to remember that sacrificial victims were not always unwilling participants. The cosmological importance of human sacrifice and bloodletting is profound at Teotihuacán and in numerable other later cities under Aztec and Maya rule. Blood sated the gods not because they were bloodthirsty in the swashbuckling sense but because all life is nourished by death. This notion of death and change is key to understanding human sacrifice in these cultures.

## The Maya and Chichén Itzá

Today the Aztec are remembered as the civilization with the vast empire, but the Mayans spread across a wide swath of land themselves. The region of Mesoamerica inhabited by the Maya stretched from the dry, flat limestone plains of the Yucatan to the wet, mountainous jungle of Chiapas and Guatemala and on to the narrow flatland of the Pacific coast. The first inhabitants of the region are believed to have been hunter gatherers, and anthropologists think these

[5] ibid.

primitive people were descended from the early migrants who moved from Asia across to the northern reaches of North America and spread south around 14000 BCE. Once settled, a more agricultural society developed in central Mexico in the 5th millennium BCE. These people were able to reliably grow crops of corn, beans and squashes through slash and burn field preparation, but depending on the quantity and quality of the soil, a field had a limited life expectancy. In some regions, particularly those where the soil cover was thin and the rainfall limited, the slash and burn technique of crop cultivation required careful attention to the seasonal weather pattern.

The ancient Mesoamericans had a worldview which was relatively flexible when it came to the addition of gods and other supernatural beings to their pantheons. Even Christianity was absorbed by the Maya as yet another divinity, and today Yucatec shamans are comfortable extorting the rain god Chaac in one breath and the Virgin Mary in the next. Thus, Kukulkan was probably worshiped alongside other deities on the Yucatan Peninsula without too much anxiety.

The *Popol Vuh* first presents the Maya version of creation by relating a series of four incarnations of men made from various materials. Unlike the Christian narrative in Genesis, the Maya creation story starts not in chaos but in a time of great quiet and stillness. The Maya gods Q'uq'umatz (the Maya version of Quetzalcoatl) and Tepeu set about creating the Earth and all its features, finally raising the sky overhead (the Sun came later). The various features of the earth are raised from sea through the conversation between the deities. The two gods then populated the Earth with all manner of animals whom they hoped would worship them, but when the animals proved unable to speak and thus worship the gods, the deities condemned them to be food for higher beings. The two gods next fashioned the first humans from mud, hoping their creation would worship them, but the mud-men dissolved before their eyes and were also unable to worship their creators. For the third attempt at creating worshippers, the tow deities enlisted the skills of the ancestral diviners Xpiyacoc and Xmucane to craft the next iteration of humans. The artisans chose wood as their medium, and though the wooden men reproduced rapidly and populated the Earth, they soon forgot their creators and refused to worship them. The gods grew tired of their ungrateful charges and sent a great flood and a rain of pitch upon them, eventually turning their cooking utensils and dogs against them.

The Maya have long been one of history's most interesting civilizations, and at the heart of the fascination is the most visited and the most spectacular of Late Classic Maya cities: Chichén Itza. Chichén Itza was inhabited for hundreds of years and was a very influential center in the later years of Maya civilization. At its height, Chichén Itza may have had over 30,000 inhabitants, and with a spectacular pyramid, enormous ball court, observatory and several temples, the builders of this city exceeded even those at Uxmal in developing the use of columns and exterior relief decoration. Of particular interest at Chichén Itza is the sacred cenote, a sinkhole that seemed to be a focus for Maya rituals around water. Since adequate supplies of water, which rarely collected on the surface of the limestone-based Yucatan Peninsula, were essential for adequate agricultural production, the Maya here considered it of primary importance. Underwater archaeology carried out in the cenote at Chichén Itza revealed that offerings to the Maya rain deity Chaac (which may have included people) were tossed into the sinkhole.

Although Chichén Itza was around for hundreds of years, it had a relatively short period of dominance in the region, lasting from about 800-950. Today, tourists are taken by guides to a building called the Nunnery for no good reason other than the small rooms reminded the Spaniards of a nunnery back home. Similarly, the great pyramid at Chichén Itza is designated *El Castillo* ("The Castle"), which it almost certainly was not, while the observatory is called *El Caracol* ("The Snail") for its spiral staircase. Of course, the actual names for these places were lost as the great Maya cities began to lose their populations, one by one. Chichén Itza was partially abandoned in 948, and the culture of the Maya survived in a disorganized way until it was revived at Mayapán around 1200. Why Maya cities were abandoned and left to be overgrown by the jungle is a puzzle that intrigues people around the world today, especially those who have a penchant for speculating on lost civilizations.

Given its importance, it is little surprise that the Feathered Serpent appears more widely in Chichén Itzá than any of the previously mentioned cities. Chichén Itzá rose to prominence around 150-200 years after the fall of both Teotihuacán and Monte Albán which might suggest one of the biggest influences these cultures had on Chichén Itzá was that of the increased religious importance of the Feathered Serpent.

The Temple of the Warriors is replete with images of Kukulkan, including great Feathered Serpent columns that still stand today. Atop this temple is a figure known as the Chacmool. This figure is seen fairly commonly throughout Mesoamerican temples. Its design is that of a recumbent man holding a bowl or having a bowl rest on his stomach as he looks out towards one side of the temple. This bowl was called a *cuauhxicalli* by the Mexica and, as well as being closely connected with the water god Tlaloc, it was the place where recently extracted human hearts were placed as offerings to the gods. It is said that all Chacmool figures depicted captured enemy warriors who bore offerings to the gods. Once again, Kukulkan/Quetzalcoatl appear surrounded by human sacrifice.

**Keith Pomakis' picture of the Temple of the Warriors**

**The Temple of the Warriors' columns**

**Bjørn Christian Tørrissen's picture of a statue of Chaac Mool located at the Temple of the Warriors**

The Feathered Serpent also appears on the round observatory at Chichén Itzá. This too has a mythological foundation since Kukulkan/Quetzalcoatl has strong associations with Venus, the Morning Star. There is a story of Kukulkan/Quetzalcoatl accompanying the sun across the sky just as the planet Venus appeared to do for the ancient Maya. Venus was associated with the Mexica water god Tlaloc, as well as the psychopomp and companion of Quetzalcoatl, Xolotl. However, after the rise and prominence of Teotihuacán, Venus was associated with warfare and the Maya planned their wars around the positioning of this planet. There is evidence of this in the so-called "Dresden Codex," which includes a Mayan calendar. In it, the Mayans recorded the movements of Venus in five cycles of 584 days. What is amazing about this is that the synodic period of Venus is actually 583.92 days.

**Daniel Schwen's picture of the observatory, El Caracol**

Perhaps the most important and famous image of the Feathered Serpent at Chichén Itzá is found only twice a year. During the spring equinox and autumn equinox, *El Castillo* (incorrectly named by the invading Spanish who mistook it for a castle/fortress) or the Temple of Kukulkan becomes a hotbed for tourists looking to see a feat of astronomically aligned architecture. When the sun strikes the temple on these days, the steps of the pyramid cast a shadow on the narrow staircase that leads to the top of the temple. Slowly, the image of a dark serpent winds its way down the steps until it meets the Feathered Serpent heads that make up the sides of the staircase. It remains one of the great intellectual and spiritual constructions of humankind, and it would not have been possible without the Maya's skill at astronomy and devotion to the Feathered Serpent.

**A picture of *El Castillo's* base, which depicts Kukulkan on the west face of the northern stairway**

Unquestionably one of the most impressive monuments in ancient Mesoamerica, *El Castillo* is a square structure that runs 60 meters (190 feet) on each side and reaches a height of 12 meters (40 feet). It is built in a step-style, like the Mesopotamian ziggurats or early Egyptian pyramids, but not like the smooth surfaces of Egyptian pyramids such as those at Giza. At the center of each of the four sides is a broad staircase, and modern climbers quickly discover the remarkable steepness of the staircase and the narrowness of the stairs themselves, which require the climber to often turn his or her feet sideways for a good footing and sometimes to lean forward, scrambling on not just feet but also hands. This was probably intended, as it would cause the devotee to clamber up in a semi-prostrate position before the might of Kukulkan.

*El Castillo* is also much broader than the typical Mayan pyramids, giving it a squat profile that is reminiscent of pyramids found around Central Mexico in places like Cholula, Tula, Teotihuacan and Tenochtitlan. The Maya often built their pyramids in stages, by sheathing a preexisting pyramid in a new layer of stone, burying the old one, and thereby creating a taller, broader replacement. Excavations by the Mexican government in the 20th century found two smaller pyramids subsumed within the current exterior. These older pyramids appeared to blend the Mayan and Toltec influences more than the last incarnation, which does away with the hybrid styles and predominantly favors the Toltec elements.[6]

**The north side of *El Castillo***

Given its prestige and the importance of rituals, it is perhaps not surprising that seemingly everyone in the city participated in much of the ritual life. *El Castillo* appears to have been designed with a broad courtyard at its base so that crowds of spectators could watch, and every kind of inhabitant would have benefited from the presence of a diverse marketplace. Moreover, many were probably proud of their citizenship in what seemed to be the world's mightiest city, and there was no better place to be devoted to the worship of the "Sovereign Plumed Serpent."

## Tollan, the "City of the Feathered Serpent"

Much of what is understood today about the Aztec religion comes from the writings of the Spanish Conquistadores, and though academics have other sources, it is the Spanish vision that shapes today's popular understanding of the Aztec. Namely, this is the idea of a sophisticated but barbaric people whose religious beliefs were based around the notion that the gods demanded

"Chichen Itza" in *Exploring Mesoamerica* by John M.D. Pohl (1999). Oxford University Press. Pgs 121

that they carve out the hearts of thousands of victims as offerings for their pleasure. Much of this picture is simply false, especially the foreigners' assumption that the gods demanded sacrifice or that it was done for the "pleasure" of the gods. This second misunderstanding shows the obvious bias of the Spanish, who had read about the Christian God of the Old Testament loving the smell of sacrifice: "Then burn the entire ram on the altar. It is a burnt offering to the Lord, a pleasing aroma, a food offering presented to the Lord." (Exo 29:18). As discussed earlier, the offerings at Aztec altars were for the subsistence of the sun and maintenance of the world, not for the gods' cruel pleasure.

One of the most important ideas at the heart of the Aztec religion was the concept of the Earth's fragility. The Aztec priests taught that the world had been destroyed and remade four times, and that they lived in the fifth and final incarnation of the world. However, unlike Christian eschatology[7], this last annihilation of the world will not result in a time of judgment and ascension to heaven, nor will it result in a sixth world. The belief was merely that this final destruction would bring about nothing but darkness and oblivion, making it a true "end of days."

Each of the previous four worlds (also translated as "ages" or "suns") had a number of aspects. First, it was not the earth that was truly remade but actually the sun that was re-ignited, so each of the "worlds" had its own named sun. Between the suns, the resident humans (or human-like creatures) would be devoured by some form of monster (such as jaguars) or transformed into some form of animal (like fish or monkeys), and the world's surface would be scoured by some calamity like hurricanes or fiery rain. Each of the worlds was presided over a single dominant deity, with Tonatiuh (the god of warriors) presiding over the current incarnation of the planet. In the table provided below, the details of each of the five worlds is laid out, including the name of the dominant god, the name of the sun in both Nahuatl (the Aztec language) and English, a description of the nature of humanity in that age, and how both the world and the human race were obliterated at the end.

In the current age, humans ate corn and lived under a sun called *Naui ollin* ("Four Movement"). At the beginning of this age, four giants were created to hold up the corners of the sky, and among them the most important was "Falling Eagle," who was a symbol of the role of the divine on the earth[8]. At the end of times, the sun would burn out and darkness would descend. At that point, celestial monsters called "tzitzimime" would descend from the heavens to devour humanity and all of the earth would be destroyed by a great earthquake.

Of course, delaying this ultimately inevitable destruction was the goal of much of the Aztec religion. The gods were understood as natural allies in defending their creation, but they were

---

7   In theology "eschatology" is those myths and ruminations that explore the end of the world and the ultimate destiny of humanity. In Christianity, eschatology is focused upon the writings of the apocryphal *Book of Revelations*.

8   "Falling Eagle" at the *Mythology Dictionary* (2013). Accessed online at:
    http://www.mythologydictionary.com/falling-eagle-mythology.html

seen as unable to delay the destruction on their own, so they needed the constant assistance of their worshipers.

**The Aztec Sequence of the Five Worlds or "Suns"[9]**

| Number of the World | Dominant God | Name of the Sun | What was the nature of the human population? | How was humanity destroyed? | How was the world destroyed? |
|---|---|---|---|---|---|
| 1 | Tezcatlipoca | Naui ocelotl ("Four Jaguar") | Giants who ate acorns | Eaten by jaguars | Destroyed by jaguars |
| 2 | Quetzalcoatl | Naui ehecatl ("Four Wind") | Humans who ate piñon nuts (acocentli) | Transformed into monkeys | Destroyed by hurricanes |
| 3 | Tlaloc | Naui quiahuitl ("Four Rain") | Humans who ate aquatic seeds (acecentli) | Transformed into dogs, turkeys and butterflies | Destroyed by a rain of fire |
| 4 | Chalchiuhtlicue | Naui atl ("Four Water") | Humans who ate wild seeds | Transformed into fish | Destroyed by a great flood |
| 5 | Tonatiuh | Naui ollin ("Four movement") | Humans who eat corn | To be eaten by celestial monsters ("tzitzimime") | Destroyed by an earthquake |

9    Chart adapted from: *The Aztec of Central Mexico: An Imperial Society 2nd ed.* by Frances F. Berdan (2005). Wadsworth, Cengage Learning Publishers.  Pgs 129

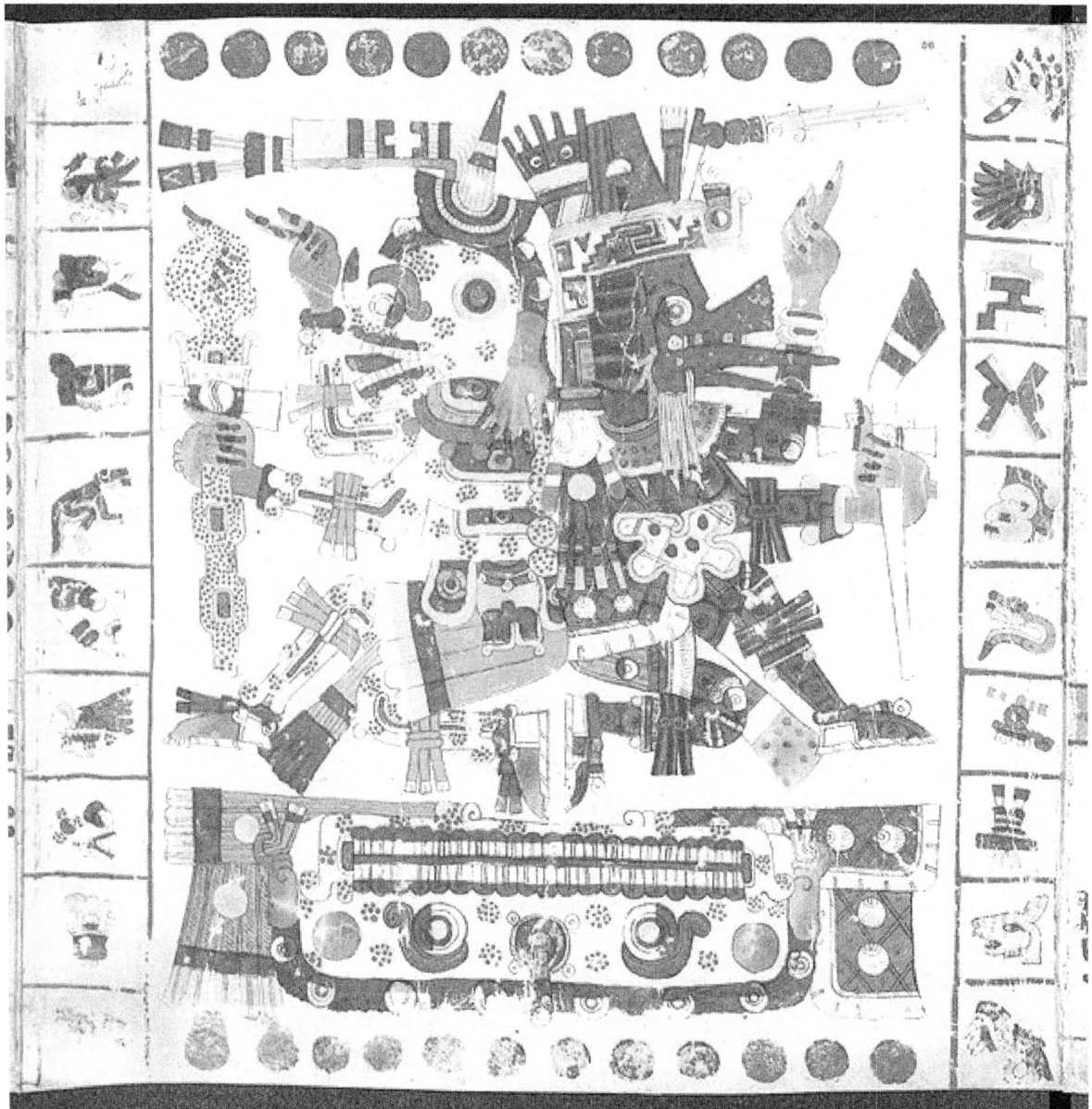

**An image depicting Mictlantecuhtli (left), the god of death and lord of the Underworld, next to Quetzalcoatl, the god of wisdom, life, knowledge, morning star, and lord of the West**

As has been previously emphasized, the Aztec Empire was a remarkably diverse spiritual landscape, which meant that hundreds if not thousands of deities and spirits of varying importance and power were worshiped and venerated throughout the Empire at the time of European contact. This also means that the deities of Mexico did not form a "tight" pantheon in the way that the Greek, Roman or Norse gods did, where the gods were all seen as having relationships to one another and the myths all revolved around their deeds. Instead, the Aztec religion's pantheon was "loose", with some gods seen as related to each other in little family clusters but others as more-or-less freestanding beings.

For the purpose of the State Religion, the most important of these gods was Huitzilopotchli. Throughout Mesoamerica, worship and maintenance of the sun was a paramount religious duty, and in most cases, this god was Tonatiuh, the Fifth Sun and the patron of this final era of the world who struggled every day to be born, cross the sky, and die again[10]. However, with the rise of Tlacaelel's revised Aztec State Faith, Tonatiuh began to be displaced from worship and replaced by the ethnic god Huitzilopotchli. Thus, it was Huitzilopotchli who received sacrifices and had a temple (along with Tlaloc) atop the Templo Mayor at the heart of Tenochtitlan. The exact relationship between the two gods is vague, but both were patrons of war and the sun (with Huitzilopotchli only adopting the sun relationship later), and it is possible that the Aztec viewed Huitzilopotchli as another name for Tonatiuh or a replacement for him or that both shared the task of lighting and warming the world.

10 "Tonatiuh" at the *Encyclopedia Britannica* (2014). Accessed online at:
   http://www.britannica.com/EBchecked/topic/599069/Tonatiuh

# A depiction of Huitzilopotchli in the Codex Telleriano-Remensis

Huitzilopotchli's name means "Hummingbird of the Left" (*huitzilin meaning* "hummingbird," and *opochtli signifying* "left"), but this direct translation misses the subtleties of the name. The Aztec believed that hummingbirds were the reincarnated souls of warriors, and they associated the left with the south and so a better translation might be "Reborn Warrior of the South." The god was said to take two forms - an eagle and a hummingbird[11] - and the altar of Huitzilopotchli carried from the north was a depiction of a hummingbird carried on the shoulders of priests who then spoke to them at night while the group had made camp to provide orders for the coming day. Similarly, it was in the form of a golden eagle killing a serpent atop a cactus that the god marked the spot where Tenochtitlan was to be founded.

Unlike Huitzilopotchli, Quetzalcoatl or even Tezcatlipoca, Tlaloc is an earthy god. The Greeks differentiated between Olympian deities who were associated with the skies and celestial objects and events and Chthonic gods who were associated with the rocks, soil and living things. In Mesoamerica, there is a similar division with the nomadic peoples of the northern deserts - the Chichimecs and their descendants the Aztec and Toltecs - worshiping gods of the stars, the moon, the sun and the skies (such as Huitzilopotchli or Quetzalcoatl) - and the long-term inhabitants of Central Mexico, the direct cultural descendents of Teotihuacán, who worshiped gods of the earth.

While Tlaloc at first appears to be a sky god, it is apparent that he is not a celestial deity like the others previously mentioned. Tlaloc is associated with the mountain tops, where the rocks were believed to have exhaled the vapors from the deeps that make up the clouds. The mountains were also believed to be the homes of his assistants, demigod figures called the Tlaloque, who were also associated with the rains[12]. Tlaloc's consort was Chalchiuhtlicue[13] ("She who wears a jade skirt"), a fellow water Goddess associated with lakes and streams, and both gods were associated with particular mountains at Teotihuacán and Tenochtitlan alike. Another god closely associated with Tlaloc was Tecciztecatl, a god of the Moon who was thought of as Tlaloc's son. He was depicted carrying a white shell on his back, much like a snail, and was associated with masculinity.[14]

11 "Huitzilopotchli" at the *Encyclopedia Britannica* (2014). Accessed online at:
   http://www.britannica.com/EBchecked/topic/275172/Huitzilopochtli
12 "Tlaloc" at the *Encyclopedia Britannica* (2014). Accessed online at:
   http://www.britannica.com/EBchecked/topic/597478/Tlaloc
13 "Chalchiuhtlicue" at the *Encyclopedia Mythica* by Micha F. Lindemans (1997). Accessed online at:
   http://www.pantheon.org/areas/mythology/americas/aztec/articles.html
14 "Tecciztecatl" at the *Encyclopedia Mythica* by Micha F. Lindemans (1997). Accessed online at:
   http://www.pantheon.org/areas/mythology/americas/a

**The depiction of Tecciztecatl in the Codex Borgia**

Tlaloc had destroyed the Second Age, which was ruled by Quetzalcoatl, with his storms, and he then created a new aqueous Third Age under a sun named "Four Rain." This age featured a species of humans that ate aquatic seeds. He would preside over the Third Age until he was finally ousted by Chalchiuhtlicue, who ruled over the Fourth Age under a sun named "Four Water."

Like Huitzilopotchli, Quetzalcoatl was considered a celestial god by the Aztec. He was the son of the star-mother Coatlicue[15] and the twin brother of Xolotl, as well as the full brother of the gods Quetzalpetlatl, Camxtoli and Huitzilopochtli himself. An alternative myth of his creation

---

15 Though the diversity of religious opinion in Mesoamerica means that his parentage was also attributed to: Mixcoatl and Xochiquetzal or Ometeotl and Ometicuhtli or Tonacatecuhtli and Tonacacihuatl, or Iztacmixcohuatl. This plethora of potential parents probably relates to the pan-Mesoamerican cult being adapted to local contexts as it spread, where local people attributed the new deity to popular local gods and goddesses.

was that he was originally an aspect or part of the sun-god Tezcatlipoca (a different form of the Toltec dark sorcerer/god) who ruled over the first sun and the first age. At the end of that first era, as celestial jaguars descended to devour humanity and scour the earth, the sun died and the lord-god Tezcatlipoca was ravaged. In the midst of this destruction, Quetzalcoatl came upon his brother and slew him, after which he recreated the sun and a new species of humans using the bones of the dead and his own blood. All agree that Quetzalcoatl ruled over the second age of the world and was a great benefactor for his people, stealing the first maize seeds from the gods while in the form of an ant and bringing them to humanity. His blessed rule lasted for 676 years before Quetzalcoatl's rival Tlaloc sent hurricanes to sweep the Earth clean (except for a few people transformed into monkeys).

At the end of his time, Quetzalcoatl immolated himself, with legends claiming he did so out of remorse for being tricked into committing incest with his sister Quetzalpetlatl or, alternatively, that he was beaten by a vengeful Tezcatlipoca and fled with his followers in a boat to the east. Those who said he was immolated say that he rose again after eight days, and all agree that he has taken the form of the planet Venus, an important celestial object throughout Mesoamerica (his rising in the east was symbolic of the direction in which he traveled).

The myths are a bit confusing at some points because Quetzalcoatl was also believed to be a living king who founded the Toltec Empire and whose capital was the legendary city of Tollan. According to this version, he was forced into exile and left Mesoamerica on a raft going east, where he was deified and became the Evening Star[16].

Quetzalcoatl is perhaps the most well-known Aztec god today because of the common myth that the Aztec believed the Spaniards were gods. This is a tale that goes back to the conquistadores themselves, who took up any opportunity to note the superstitious and religiously backward nature of their enemies. This myth has pervaded popular imagination so thoroughly that one text written to help children understand the Spanish Conquest asserted, "The Aztec decided it was time for the Spanish to leave. They did not want to kill them because they might be gods after all, but the Aztec wanted them to move along."

In reality, the division between human and god was a somewhat fluid one for the Aztec (Quetzalcoatl was a man who became a god), and they believed that some humans possessed abilities that were of a divine origin, such as priests who spoke to the gods and delivered their messages to humanity. It is possible that they viewed the Spaniards in a similar manner, but it must be remembered that they also viewed themselves in this light and saw no contradiction with two different groups being chosen by divine beings for their own purposes. Therefore, the Aztec at the time of the Spanish Conquest were most definitely not paralyzed by fear that their new visitors were Aztec gods.

---

16 "Quetzalcoatl" at the *Mythology Dictionary* (2013). Accessed online at:
http://www.mythologydictionary.com/quetzalcoatl-mythology.html

Acclaimed historian and anthropologist David Carrasco described the fabled city of Tollan as the "City of the Feathered Serpent" thanks to the oral history passed down by the Aztec during and after the Spanish Conquest. The Aztec told their new masters about this place, and Bernadino de Sahagún was a Franciscan friar who took it upon himself to interview elders in the Aztec community just after the conquest in 1521. He spent the better part of the years ca.1530-1570 recording every aspect of culture he could learn from the local inhabitants and, despite the fact that many Spaniards saw his activities as contrary to their aims and ambitions in the region, much of his 12-volume *Florentine Codex* survives to this day.

In the *Florentine Codex*, Tollan is described as a glorious kingdom inhabited by the great "Toltec" people and governed by a famous priest-king called Topiltzin-Quetzalcoatl (translated as "Our Young Prince, the Plumed Serpent").[17] The stories of Topiltzin-Quetzalcoatl were those of utopian ideals. The people were wise, crops grew to Brobdingnagian proportions, and the organization of the city was the archetype of the Aztec ideal: "The Toltec house … consisted of four abodes. One was facing east: this was the house of gold; that which served as the stucco was gold plate joined to it. One was facing west, toward the setting sun; this was the house of green stone, the house of fine turquoise … One was facing south, toward the irrigated lands, this was the house of shells or of silver … one was facing north, toward the plains … this was the red house; red because red shells were inlaid in the interior walls."[18] The four-petaled flower formation imitated and channeled the forces of the cosmos for the good of the city. Every brick was laid to an exact angle based on centuries of astrological and cosmological observation and study out of which was born a worldview that the Aztec brought to life in their art and architecture.

The art and stories told of Tollan imitate the vast amount of material record found across Mesoamerica concerning Quetzalcoatl, and one of the natives interviewed said the following about him: "Truly with him it began, truly from him it flowed out, from Quetzalcoatl, all art and knowledge."[19] Quetzalcoatl was at the birth of the cosmos and was responsible for such inventions as sculpture, turquoise-working, and the calendar that governed every aspect of Aztec life. Quetzalcoatl's stories often include him as being a real man, a legendary invader, a demigod, a god, and a cunning force of creation, but either way, he was always at the heart of much of Aztec culture.

### Stories of the Feathered Serpent

With the onset of the so-called Classic Period (ca. 250–1000 CE) the Feathered Serpent appeared in more art across Mesoamerica, so it should be no surprise that he was associated with more stories and more roles in local mythology.

---

[17] Carrasco 2012
[18] ibid.
[19] ibid.

One of the most important texts for these cosmographies is the Mayan *Popol Vuh*. This book begins with a declaration of how it is a "demonstration, revelation and account of how things were put in shadow and brought to light by the Maker, Modeller, named Bearer and Begetter, Hunahpu Possum, Hunahpu Coyote, Great White Peccary, Tapir, *Sovereign Plumed Serpent,* Heart of the Lake, Heart of the Sea, Maker of the Blue-Green Plate, Maker of the Blue-Green Bowl."[20] Here the Feathered Serpent appears at the dawn of time wearing his mantle as "Sovereign," and his appearance is not just limited to the Mayan version of the creation of the cosmos.

Although the *Popol Vuh* is undoubtedly the richest and, by modern standards, the fullest "story" to come out of the Mesoamerican cultures, it is not the only version by any means. There is a Nahua version to be found in the "Legend of the Suns" in the *Codex Chimalpopoca*, a Mexica/Aztec codex that documents the pre-Colombian history of central Mexico and also describes the Mexica/Aztec cosmology. The Nahua people are the direct descendants of the Mexica, and it is known that their language, Nahuatl, has been in continuous use since that time.[21] In the Nahua version of events, there are Five Ages, the fifth being the age the Mexica believed they were living in.

The first four Ages were described in quick succession in the Legend of the Suns. After the gods divide the earth among them, the sun holds power for two and a half millennia before the First Age arrives. This age was called 4 Jaguar (actually the name of a date as it was customary to use dates for names)[22], and the humans that lived during this age ate 7 Grass for their food. Although it's unknown what exactly is meant by the name "7 Grass," the names of the ages are of particular importance since they refer to the date and method of destruction that age faced. In the case of 7 Jaguar, it was believed that ferocious jaguars consumed it on the day it was prophesied they would, 676 years after its commencement. The Second Age was called 4 Wind, it lasted 364 years and it was inhabited by monkeys who ate 12 Snake and transformed into Turkeys so they could survive the destructive winds that would consume them. The Third Age was called 4 Rainstorm; it lasted just 312 years before it was consumed on the day of its name. According to the text, the turkeys that survived the Third Age turned themselves into human "Nobles" at the end of their age which was brought about by a great "rain of fire" sent down from a volcano. The Fourth Age was called 4 Water; it lasted for 676 years, during which time the Nobles ate 4 Flower and subsequently had to turn themselves into fish in order to escape the flood that destroyed the world.

There is a wonderfully resilient aspect to this story that is often smothered by other stories of the Mexica/Aztec. In this Nahua version, humans survive (albeit in different forms) the disasters that keep coming around, so the deadly cycle of creation and destruction is thwarted by human

---

[20] See Read 2000
[21] ibid.
[22] Knight 2012

ingenuity and adaptation. Within this story is another common occurrence in Mesoamerican myth: the number four. In the Mayan version of events, there are four ages, and in the Nahua version there were four previous ages before the age of the people who created it. The cosmos divided into four, there were four Cardinal Directions, and there were four petals on the flower.

What's also very important is the length of each Age and the date on which it was destroyed. The Aztec lived their lives and constructed their cities according to the mathematics that governed the stars. There is no wonder, then, that their cosmology would put equal importance on this system. Every day on the calendar was of importance, so the day a child was born would determine the child's name and also a regime to be followed by their parents, and the children themselves, of which the aim was to enhance that day's auspicious benefits to the child's personality and/or life, and to be wary of the potential pitfalls being born on that day would create for them.[23]

What is curious about the Fifth Age is that the gods set about creating a new set of humans in the form of an "ideal couple." It would seem that, in the Nahua tradition, not even the gods' plans are always successful, however. The first couple were called Tata and Nene, and they were created just before the waters came to destroy the end of the world. The great god Titlacahuan-Tezcatlipoca asked them what he could do for them, and they replied that they wanted him to drill a hole in the cypress tree and to put them in it until the waters subsided. The god did so and gave them a cob of corn each to eat while they waited.

When the waters subsided and Tata and Nene knew it was safe, they left the cypress tree and lit a fire to roast some fish. But this was not appreciated by the gods. The smoke from the fire blackened the sky, so Titlacahuan-Tezcatlipoca scolded them for what they had done, cut off their heads, and sewed them back onto their buttocks, thus making them the first dogs in the age of the Fifth Sun.[24]

Once the first dogs had been created, the gods all gathered together and wondered who would finally be the masters of the lands they had created for the Fifth Age. Quetzalcoatl was one of these worried gods, and he set about finding a solution. The first thing he did was travel to Mictlan, the Land of the Dead, and speak to its Lord and Lady, Mictlantecuhtli and Mictlancihuatl. He told them that he had come for the greenstone bones that they were guarding, and that he wished to take them with him. Distrusting Quetzalcoatl, Mictlantecuhtli asked what he was going to do with them, to which Quetzalcoatl replied that the gods were unhappy about an uninhabited Earth and that he wished to use the greenstone bones to repopulate it. But Mictlantecuhtli was either not in favor of the idea of repopulation or simply didn't want to be robbed of his precious greenstone bones, so he set Quetzalcoatl the impossible task of blowing a conch-shell horn that had no holes in it. If he could do that, he was welcome to take the bones

---

[23] See Carrasco 2012 for an excellent description of this.
[24] See Read 2000 for a wonderfully elaborate version of these events.

with him.

Like any good trickster, Quetzalcoatl had a trick up his sleeve. He secretly spoke to the worms and bumblebees and the honeybees of the land and asked for their help. They answered his call and burrowed holes into the conch-shell as Quetzalcoatl blew into it with success.

Mictlantecuhtli pretended to relent when he heard the sound of the horn, but when Quetzalcoatl went to take the greenstone bones, he was confronted by the Micteca, the people of the Land of the Dead, who told him he had to leave the bones in Mictlan. Quetzalcoatl, seeing that he had been betrayed, retreated in quiet contemplation, during which time his *Nahualli* - or "spirit animal" in the shamanistic sense, to define it roughly - spoke to him and simply told him to lie. Quetzalcoatl called out to Mictlantecuhtli, saying that he was going to leave the bones, but instead he scooped them up and left.

When he picked up the bones, Quetzalcoatl paid no heed to how they lay in Mictlan and so he mixed them up, mixing male bones and female bones as he ran with them in a bundle. Mictlantecuhtli soon realized Quetzalcoatl's trick and called to the Micteca and ordered them to dig a pit before the entrance to the Land of the Living. True to Mictlantecuhtli's desires, Quetzalcoatl tumbled headfirst into the pit, knocked himself unconscious, and the greenstone bones were strewn about the pit. A group of quails entered the pit and began chewing and breaking up the bones while Quetzalcoatl was unconscious. When he awoke, he turned to his *Nahualli* and asked what will come of the bones after this, to which his *Nahualli* told him he had messed up and "what will be will be."

Quetzalcoatl brushed himself off, gathered up the bones, and continued running all the way to Tamoanchan, where he gave them to Cihuacoatl - a goddess of motherhood - and begged for her help. Cihuacoatl took the greenstone bones and ground them up in a greenstone bowl. Then Quetzalcoatl came along and cut his genitalia and let it bleed into the bowl. Then the gods came and "gave them merit,"[25] and, from then on, the "commoners" of the world lived because of this "merit" and the blood Quetzalcoatl spilled for them.

There are a few important aspects of this story from a mythological standpoint. The first is that of Quetzalcoatl's role as a trickster. Tricksters are very often what is called "culture heroes" meaning that they - whether they intended to be or not - are responsible for the invention of certain things or aspects of the world as seen by the cultures who worshipped them. There are many of these characters in all cultures around the world. For example, the Norse god Loki invented the fishing net when he was trying to imagine how the other gods might catch him, and the Greek god Hermes invented the lyre in order to get himself out of trouble with Zeus after stealing Apollo's herd. The Native American spirit-god Raven, in the Tsimshian cycle, comes to the dark earth from the heavens where there is light and subsequently returns to steal the light

---

[25] See Read 2000

and bring it to the humans.[26]

Tricksters create things and often create other things by accident. By falling into the pit created by the Mictlan, Quetzalcoatl performs another action of the trickster, that of making mistakes. Tricksters are not infallible gods (a notion invented and clung to by much later civilizations), and it is often their failings that become fortuitous happenstance, as is the case of his falling into the pit and breaking up and mixing the bones. His connection with his *Nahualli* and other animals of the world, as is the case in the scene with the conch-shell, is another example of Quetzalcoatl being a trickster as tricksters are often dependent on other animals or spirits in the world. They are individualistic but do not live in a vacuum, and their interests and curiosity only exist in tandem with some devious antagonist or some unfortunate victim of their schemes.

What's important in the story of Quetzalcoatl and the first "common" humans is blood. The most important substance for the Aztec's religious beliefs was human blood. Across Mesoamerica, the sacrifice of human blood was a central feature of religious ritual, and it was the blood sacrifice of Jesus - so vividly depicted in the colonial churches of Mexico and Guatemala that it can disturb modern visitors - that resonated strongly with the new Catholic converts. While the live human sacrifices performed at the most important temples caught the attention of the Europeans and gave justification for conquests they already intended to achieve, all practitioners of the Aztec religion regularly gave of their own blood in rituals. Moreover, it was not only human blood that animated and empowered; according to myth, the serpent god Quetzalcoatl recreated humanity at the beginning of the Third Age by pouring out his own blood over the bones of the people of the Second Age. The gods are regularly described offering part of their life essence in the form of blood to transform the world or to empower suns.

It's well known that the Aztec practiced human sacrifice, but a common misconception is the scale on which they did so. Human sacrifice was far less common than bloodletting performed by willing agents.[27] Stingray spines and thorns were often used to pierce the tongue or other body parts so that blood could flow into a bowl or onto an altar. This may appear macabre today, but in conjunction with the stories about Quetzalcoatl, there is a certain logic to it for those who earnestly believed the stories. The Aztec were offering their own blood by way of imitating the sacrifice Quetzalcoatl made for them.

There is also an aspect of time that must be mentioned in this respect. To the Aztec, blood was life, and death was a very real and inevitable part of the cycle of human activities. This word, cycle, is key to understanding much of Aztec lore and practice. Bloodletting fed the lifeforce initiated by the gods and had to be done on a cyclical basis because time did not move in a straight line but in cycles. What Quetzalcoatl began the day he stole the greenstone bones, those made from the greenstone bones would have to be mindful to repeat, lest the life-force become

---

[26] See Hyde 2008
[27] Carrasco 2012

diminished in the world.

The gods met at Teotihuacán before the Fifth Sun was created. There the gods came together and asked each other who would give the world dawn, and who would become and carry the sun through the heavens for the first day of the Fifth Age, the age of nobles and commoners. They were hesitant because, although it was an honor, that honor came at the ultimate price. There was silence at Teotihuacán until Tecuciztecatl stepped forward and volunteered.

Then the gods asked who would become the moon. They asked and asked but nobody rose to the call. They turned to Nanahuatzin, who was standing meekly, listening to what the rest of the gods said, and they said, "You, you shall become the moon." After that, Nanahuatzin agreed. He stepped forward and told the gods that it would be his honor to become the moon.

And so they were chosen, and they prepared for the ceremony by fasting for four days together. After they fasted, Tecuciztecatl and Nanahuatzin gathered around the fire pit they called the "God Oven."[28] The rest of the gods bestowed riches and finery upon Tecuciztecatl. He had ritual branches made of quetzal feathers, a heart of woven gold, a spine of greenstone and a bloodletting instrument made of coral. Meanwhile, Nanahuatzin was given ritual branches of green grass and reeds, a grass ball made of pine needles and his bloodletting instrument was a humble maguey thorn. And where they had been preparing two mountains, two pyramid-mountains rose out of the ground and stand there to this day: the Sun Pyramid and the Moon Pyramid.

After four nights of celebration, Tecuciztecatl and Nanahuatzin dashed their preparatory objects to the ground and the gods gave Tecuciztecatl a headdress made of egret, but to Nanahuatzin they gave only paper. When midnight arrived, the gods made a procession around the God Oven and then lined up on either side of Tecuciztecatl and Nanahuatzin before the fire. But Tecuciztecatl hesitated. The gods reprimanded him and shouted at him, but still he would not move. They called out to him to jump, to throw himself into the fire so as to be a sacrifice and to create the sun and the sun god out of himself, but Tecuciztecatl could not move. He was frozen before the God Oven. Every time he looked at the fire, he grew more daunted by it. He tried four times to sacrifice himself but could not summon the courage until, once again, the gods were forced to summon Nanahuatzin.

Humble Nanahuatzin stepped up to the fire and his courage did not fail him. He closed his eyes calmly and then stepped into the flames. He lay down among them and his flesh began to burn and crack, but he did not cry out. When Tecuciztecatl saw Nanahuatzin boldly rise to the honor that should have been his, he also threw himself into the fire and there they burned together. Then, out of the flames, flew a glorious eagle with feathers the color of evenly singed wings. After the eagle, the fire shifted and out strode the jaguar, scorched unevenly because of the

---

[28] ibid.

shifted stones. Due to their bravery, especially that of Nanahuatzin, from then on the Mexica/Aztec called the brave "eagle-jaguar" because Nanahuatzin the eagle was bravest and therefore deserved to open the naming.

Then the gods waited for the dawn. They lay by the fire looking in all the four directions until they saw the sky turn red like the blending of a dye, and soon enough Nanahuatzin rose as the first sun into the sky, blazing and warming the land as it rested above them. Then Tecuciztecatl, as another sun, rose into the sky and followed Nanahuatzin's course, but it too stopped in the sky. The gods grew nervous, one of them ran to Tecuciztecatl and beat the sun with a rabbit and killed it, yet still it would not move. This is when the rest of the gods knew that Tecuciztecatl and Nanahuatzin's sacrifices were not enough, and they determined they all needed to die. Quetzalcoatl-Ehecatl stepped forward and killed the gods, including Xolotl, who tried to escape his fate.

When Quetzalcoatl-Ehecatl had killed the gods, he turned to the suns and still they would not move in the sky, so Quetzalcoatl-Ehecatl knew what he had to do. He stood up straight, gathered all of his strength, and heaved vast amounts of air into his cavernous chest and blew on the sun. Then the sun moved and the moon moved, and they took up the path that they still follow to this day.

This story is another example of the rationale behind human sacrifice and bloodletting. To the Aztec, it was the gods who sacrificed themselves so that the sun and the moon could be created. Also, like the sun and moon, this act of sacrifice-creation would need to be repeated ad infinitum if humans wanted the cycle to continue. The importance of voluntarily sacrificing one's life for the greater good is also apparent here. Tecuciztecatl had the chance to gain the greatest honor for the gods - that of becoming the life-bringing sun - but because of his cowardice, he was relegated to the role of the moon, the "dead" sun that was beaten and defaced. It is documented that there were voluntary human sacrifices, but many of them were also captured soldiers. Scholars have discovered evidence that those soldiers who were chosen to be sacrificed partook in ceremonies over the course of several days, including dancing and feasting. These soldiers were expected to face their deaths like Nanahuatzin so that they could take their place in the great cycle of life and death.

The Quetzalcoatl of this story is a much more solemn character than that in the story about the birth of humankind. He is referred to as Quetzalcoatl-Ehecatl in this story because this is Quetzalcoatl's manifestation as a god of the wind. In this he is closely connected with Tlaloc, the god of the rain, and he often appears in similar iconography. What's most important about Quetzalcoatl's role here, however, is that of the prime mover. He took it upon himself to sacrifice the gods when the sun would not move, and when he saw that wasn't enough to set things in motion, he mustered his own magical strength in order to do so. The sun and the moon were the foci of the heavens, and, for a culture so interested in astronomy, their movements were paramount. Therefore, this act of Quetzalcoatl's would have been seen as no small act to an agricultural people that put such importance on the changing of the seasons.

At Teotihuacán, the Feathered Serpent sprawled its body through maritime imagery and seemingly contrasted with a warlike fiery god. If the Feathered Serpent and the "Fiery God" do - as some scholars suggest - represent the two seasons of the year, then Quetzalcoatl's association with agriculture can be traced back to this great culture. As one scholar brilliantly put it, the dry season was for feeding the gods (with bloody wars) while the wet season was for feeding the people.[29] That Quetzalcoatl instigated the cycle that governed these seasons was not enough as he was also given the honour of being the rain-bearing wind too.

Due to the fact that very little epigraphical evidence from the time of Teotihuacán has been found, it's very difficult to understand how these cultures viewed Quetzalcoatl's predecessors, the Feathered Serpents. However, it is known that the Mayan word for *serpent* was the same word they used for *sky* so it's likely that he was considered a celestial deity from the earliest usages of the Mayan languages. Given that the leaders of Mesoamerican cultures were often granted/expected to uphold the traditions that facilitated the rain-bearing winds, there was a connection between Quetzalcoatl and nobility too. For this connection, one may look to the Temple of the Feathered Serpent at Teotihuacán again where there is evidence of a noble interment (sadly looted many years ago) that suggests this temple may have housed other noble's tombs also.[30]

There is a story that reflects Quetzalcoatl's association with the elements that provide food for the people. Firstly, it's important to note that the Mexica believed the mountains and potable water to be intrinsically connected, most probably due to the fast flowing streams that came down the slopes and were used in their vast irrigation projects. As the story goes, when the commoners were first created in the Fifth Age, the gods were pondering what this new creation should eat. At that point Quetzalcoatl saw an ant walking along carrying a kernel of corn. Quetzalcoatl questioned the ant who did his very best to ignore the god and keep on his merry way but Quetzalcoatl was insistent so eventually the ant gave up and pointed to what was called the Mountain of Produce. Quetzalcoatl turned to look at the mountain, then transformed himself into a black ant and made his way to the mountain and brought a kernel of corn back to the gods at Tamoanchan. They asked Quetzalcoatl what they should do with this mountain. The humans wouldn't be able to access the corn as they were not shapeshifters like Quetzalcoatl. Quetzalcoatl tried to carry the mountain to Tamoanchan on his back but he wasn't capable. So, two of the gods, Oxomoco and Cipactonal, took the kernels of corn they had and began casting lots with them as the shamans did and have done for centuries. Their casting revealed the answer to them: they would call on Nanahuatzin, the Old Thunder-Bolt, to crack the mountain open which he did and all the other rain gods came and stole away all the corn so they could divest them to the

---

[29] Read 2000
[30] ibid.

humans another day.

As Read noted, Quetzalcoatl's relationship with the other rain gods is an obvious one. The wind moves the clouds, which produce the rain, which irrigates the land, which was the chief currency and expression of power. In all of the surviving documents from the Mexica culture, it is their vast empire of tributes that is lauded above and beyond any other cultural aspect. Wagonloads of corn were mentioned among the gold and worked materials that added to the riches of the Mexica nobles. Once again, Quetzalcoatl appears involved with nobility and the "correct" order and maintenance of the universe.

Some scholars believe that the end of the great civilization at Tula had its seeds sown in religious discord. The Nonoalca and the Tolteca-Chichimeca groups were distinct ethnic groups whose cultural expression is distinct in the material record. Such divisions led to a legend arising that speaks of the fall of Tula in terms of a great battle between two gods: Tezcatlipoca and Quetzalcoatl.

Tezcatlipoca was one of the gods who sent Quetzalcoatl to the Land of the Dead to get the greenstone bones and also one of those who eventually sacrificed himself in the God Oven; however, his relationship with Quetzalcoatl is a complex one. Kay A. Read gives a magnificently concise description of Tezcatlipoca's attributes: "As a god of the night sun, the night wind, and the cosmos's four waters (each of which was controlled by one of his four aspects), he played a key role in cosmic creation; oversaw life events both good and bad; educated people and passed judgment on their actions; controlled success in war; legitimated and deligitimated Mexica rulership; and by the end of the Conquest, to some he had become the Devil himself."[31] The initial attributes may seem familiar after reading the earlier parts of this book. It is indeed true that Tezcatlipoca, though not a minor god by any means, did adopt many of the attributes of Quetzalcoatl in the later years of the Mexica. By the time the Spanish arrived, he had become such a prevalent deity that the Spanish felt the need to vilify him.

The antagonism between Tezcatlipoca and Quetzalcoatl goes way back to the beginning of time, according to the Mexica version of events. It is said that Tezcatlipoca ruled over the first of the five Ages but Quetzalcoatl, out of either brotherly animosity or jealousy, knocked Tezcatlipoca out of the sky and, as a result, Tezcatlipoca returned in the form of a jaguar that destroyed the world. Quetzalcoatl restarted the world after him and ruled over it until Tezcatlipoca returned as the god of the "Night Wind" and destroyed the world again. This is one reason why some scholars have speculated that Tezcatlipoca was the embodiment of change through violence.[32] Another reason for this attribution is the history the Mexica told of the "real" rulers Tezcatlipoca and Quetzalcoatl.

---

[31] 2000
[32] Miller & Taub 1993

## Man vs. Myth

According to Mexica tradition, Chichén Itzá was invaded by an exiled ruler known as the Feathered Serpent. This ruler had come from Tula, which was considered the greatest artistic civilization to that date and so, after he took over Chichén Itzá from the native Itzá tribe, he instigated the greatest artistic and architectural advances that culture had ever enjoyed. This is a common notion among the Mexica whose many myths all tend to refer to themselves as being invaders from the north, establishing and taking the greatest cities in Mesoamerica.

The veracity of such a story is difficult to pin down, however. Much of what is known of this Feathered Serpent invader comes from post-Conquest sources. Kay A. Read, once again, breaks the problem down concisely, and that there are four issues with it. Firstly, that the sources are not only late but they're also fragmented and are not necessarily related to each other. Secondly, the interpretation of said texts are very loose and can, in fact, be interpreted in different ways that don't necessarily land upon the Feathered Serpent being the invading force that revolutionised Chichén Itzá. Thirdly, if the Toltec exiles came from a much greater, much more artistically accomplished civilization than the Itzá, then why are the constructions at Chichén Itzá so much more accomplished than those found in Tula? And lastly, it's so difficult to distinguish distinct architectural styles at Chichén Itzá. Yes, there are certainly Toltec influences, but these can easily be explained by comparing modern cities' variety of Neoclassical, Rococo, Baroque, Gothic and any other artistic style that is not necessarily "native" to that city. Humans around the world copy and imitate the styles they appreciate the most.[33] What is most likely to be the case is that the Mexica glorified the inhabitants and the invaders of both Tula and Chichén Itzá to such a degree that this myth unfolded out of a non-existent "Golden Age" thanks to mythological imagination and loose memories of a peripatetic past.

Quetzalcoatl performed a vital function in this respect for the Mexica as a civilization. According to the myth, the Toltec city of Tula was ruled over by Quetzalcoatl until his "political enemies" in the form of Tezcatlipoca ousted him. This appears to have been the case in the real world too as the Colhua royal line at Tula was also ousted by their political enemies which was to have an enormous impact on the political balance of the region. Towards the end of the 14th century, the first "Chief Speaker of Mexica" - the *tlatoani,* the official title of the leader of the Mexica henceforth - was Lord Acamapichtli, and it was during his reign that the Mexica truly became a political entity in their own right. Until that time, the Mexica were still the "outsiders" to the area and were struggling to throw off the yoke of nearby Azcapotzalco. However, Lord Acamapichtli was the son of a nobleman from the Colhua people and his mother was a Mexica princess. By ascending to the Mexica leadership, Lord Acamapichtli united two formidable cultures with an ethos that would remain henceforth as a fundamental pillar of Mexica culture: militarism.

---

[33] 2000

The Toltec city of Tula still bears the marks of this aspect in its iconography and material remains. Skull racks, on which were skewered the skulls of sacrificed enemy warriors, as well as the bloody *Chacmool* statues and the vast amount of predatory beast symbolism all highlight the Toltec affinity for violence.[34] This runs in tandem with the religious changes felt at Tula, where images of the antagonistic gods Quetzalcoatl and Tezcatlipoca were slowly but emphatically integrated into the architecture that had, before then, been the principal domain of the rain god Tlaloc.[35]

The increase in militarism and the more violent symbolism that came with it appears to have been a result of the invading tribes from the north, notably the Mexica striving for political independence. In the form of Lord Acamapichtli, the unification of Mexica and Toltec civilizations was also seen as the incorporation of the Toltec god Quetzalcoatl into the Mexica tradition, not necessarily supplanting the principal deity, Huitzilopochtli, but endowing Mexica leaders with the dual identity of Quetzalcoatl-Tezcatlipoca from then on.

### The Spanish

Perhaps one of the most ignominious stories of Quetzalcoatl comes from the *Codex Chimalpopoca*. This codex - evidently lost at some point during the 20th century but thoroughly studied by the German scholar Walter Lehmann before its loss - gives a brief account of some of the deities of the Mexica, written in Spanish by a 16th century or 17th century cleric. Given the late writing of this section, scholars look upon it with a certain skepticism, but the Codex Chimalpopoca contains stories of the *Legend of the Suns* that bear such a resemblance to the Mayan *Popol Vuh* that they tend to take its contents at face value and assume it to be a fairly honest account of Mexica religion.

In the *Codex Chimalpopoca* is the story of Quetzalcoatl's final days on earth. As the story goes, Quetzalcoatl traveled to the land where the sun rises in the year 1 Reed (reportedly 895 CE) because he knew he was going to die that day, just as he had been born on that day, and wished it to take place in this land. This came about after Quetzalcoatl grew discontented with the practice of human sacrifice. When the other gods heard this, they gathered together and Tezcatlipoca ordered them to make pulque (the alcoholic beverage made from fermented sap of the maguey plant still drunk today) so that Quetzalcoatl would lose his senses and fail to even perform his own bloodletting for the good of humanity and the gods.

When Quetzalcoatl arrived in the land where the sun rises, Tezcatlipoca arrived there too, bearing the pulque and a large mirror. Tezcatlipoca told the priest, who was keeping guard of Quetzalcoatl, to tell the god a young man had arrived to see him, to "give and show him his body."[36] When the priests said this to Quetzalcoatl, however, he was confused. What could

---

[34] Knight 2012
[35] ibid.
[36] See "Readings in Classical Nahuatl: The Death of Quetzalcoatl by D. K. Jordan

"show him his body" possibly mean? So Quetzalcoatl told the priests to go back to the youth and tell him to show them what he would show Quetzalcoatl. But Tezcatlipoca refused and demanded that the priests allow him access to the god.

The priests allowed him through and Tezcatlipoca gave the god salutations and declared that he was his lowly servant and had brought him a gift. Quetzalcoatl admired the young man's effort in traveling so far to greet him and asked to see the thing the youth had brought. When Tezcatlipoca revealed the mirror, Quetzalcoatl was horrified at the sight of his own body. "If my followers see this they will be horrified too," he said in shock, because "he had eyebrows completely puffed up, and eye sockets all pushed in; his face was covered with pockmarks. He was not pretty to look at."[37]

When he heard this, Tezcatlipoca went away and soon came some of the other gods who had conspired with Tezcatlipoca, and they laughed and mocked Quetzalcoatl. When Coyotlinahual, the Feather Artisan, heard of this mistreatment, he ran to Quetzalcoatl's need and addressed him, advising him to go out and let his subjects see him. Quetzalcoatl was clearly dubious about this plan but Coyotlinahual offered to adorn the god and so Quetzalcoatl agreed. First, Coyotlinahual created a feather shield and other draping clothes, then he gave Quetzalcoatl a mask made of turquoise, and then he painted his lips read and his eye sockets yellow. He gave him serpent's fangs and a beard of the turquoise bird tipped with flamingo feathers and made it long so it could be tucked in far below his chin.

Coyotlinahual held up another mirror to show Quetzalcoatl his new finery and Quetzalcoatl was impressed. So much so that he took Coyotlinahual's advice and went out so that his subjects could see him. When he had left, Coyotlinahual went to the other conspiring gods and told them that Quetzalcoatl had left and that their time had come to follow him. They did and they arrived at Quetzalcoatl's house in Tula but once again they were faced with guards unwilling to let them enter. They returned three times before one of the guards asked them from whence they had come and they replied that they had come from the great Toltec mountain, Tlamacazapa, which Quetzalcoatl heard and told his guards to let these pious men pass.

They entered and gave them the vegetables and green chilis they had brought for him, but they found him fasting and unwilling to try the pulque they had brought. "It is a libation, sire, place your finger in the liquid and taste it, it is good and strong," they said. Quetzalcoatl did this and agreed that it was fresh and he drank. Then he drank again and his new friends pushed three more servings onto Quetzalcoatl. When the god drank it, the others gave the pulque to the servants until everyone in the house was drunk.

Quetzalcoatl told the gods to bring his sister, Quetzalpetatl, to join him so they could get drunk together. The gods went to find Quetzalpetatl at the Hill of Nonhualco and told her that her

---

[37] ibid.

penitent brother wished for her to join him. When she agreed, she went to Quetzalcoatl's house and there she and her servants also "took their libations" and were soon all drunk. When this happened, however, brother and sister and the rest of the servants no longer claimed to be doing penance, their piety left them, they no longer descended to the river nor did they pierce their tongues with thorns; they did nothing about their penance until dawn.

When they all woke, they were filled with shame and Quetzalcoatl finally resolved that he should waste no more time on this mortal plane, so he asked his servants to prepare for him a great stone chest. When they did this, he lay down in it and they carried him to the sea. When they arrived there, he put on all of his finery again, cried and prepared himself to stand in the fire. The flames tore through his feathered finery and soon there was nothing left of Quetzalcoatl other than his ashes, which rose into the air and onwards into the sky. When the ashes reached the sky, all the rarest birds in the world flew up with them in a medley of colors the likes of which had never been seen before, until Quetzalcoatl's ashes turned into the star that is seen at dawn. And there he will stay until the day of his return.

According to the story above, Quetzalcoatl only lived 53 years, and, before he immolated himself, he ordered his servants to remove all evidence of his reign on Earth. This would suggest that the Quetzalcoatl recorded in the *Codex Chimalpopoca* is a mortal man rather than a god. Stating that Quetzalcoatl and Quetzalpetatl "did nothing until dawn" has been interpreted by scholars to mean that they had committed incest and it was for this reason that Quetzalcoatl finally left the earthly plane, but the references to not "descending to the river" or "piercing their tongues with spines" appear to be simple references to impiety rather than explicit references to incest. That being said, the text is slippery on this matter so it might be correct to err on the side of euphemism.

An interesting point about Quetzalcoatl's rival - although Quetzalcoatl does not even appear to recognize him in this text - is that his name, Tezcatlipoca, actually means "smoky mirror." The nomenclature blends the mortal and divine aspects of the story as much as Quetzalcoatl's end in the sky as the "Morning Star" does. Whether or not the Aztec people believed Quetzalcoatl was a human and one of their ancestral leaders is difficult to verify with the sources at hand today. However, what is known is that during and especially after the arrival of the conquistadores, the line between human and divine was blurred again.

After arriving in the Valley of Mexico, Cortés attacked the large city of Cholula, massacred many of its 100,000 inhabitants, and burned it down, destroying perhaps as many as 365 temples. He then marched to the Aztec city of Tenochtitlan, impressively situated on an island in Lake Texcoco. When his men arrived at the lakeshore they were astounded at the sight, and Cortés was ultimately greeted by emissaries of the Aztec king, Montezuma II, and invited to enter his great city of Tenochtitlan. Whether Montezuma was fearful of a repeat of the butchery at Cholula (as Cortés had planned) or, as was reported in the Aztec account of the event, he thought Cortés was an incarnation of Quetzalcoatl, the hospitality Montezuma offered to the Spanish was ill-advised. The Aztec king made a second error by putting up his guests in the palace Axayácatl. Wandering about the magnificent guest quarters, the conquistadores discovered a room full of treasures.

The hostility towards the Aztec religion began immediately upon the Spaniards' arrival. In writing home about his reaction upon entering the Templo Mayor, Cortés describes his first acts of vandalism: "In these chapels are the images or idols, although, as I have before said, many of them are also found on the outside; the principal ones, in which the people have greatest faith and confidence, I precipitated from their pedestals, and cast them down the steps of the temple, purifying the chapels in which they had stood, as they were all polluted with human blood, shed in the sacrifices. In the place of these I put images of Our Lady and the Saints, which excited not a little feeling in Muteczuma and the inhabitants."[38]

With their appetite whetted by the sight of treasure, the Spaniards began to spoil for conflict, and the eager conquistadores soon found their excuse when they interrupted an Aztec religious ceremony, and, appalled by the sight of human sacrifice, massacred the Aztecs in the main temple of Tenochtitlan. In the subsequent riot, Montezuma who, by this time was being held hostage by the Spanish, was paraded before his subjects to quell the unrest. Whether he was killed by a rock thrown by one of his own people or murdered by a Spanish soldier is still unclear, but upon his death the riot turned even uglier. Cortés and his troops viciously fought their way out of Tenochtitlan and crossed a causeway to the mainland. They then laid siege to the Aztec city, cutting off the food supply.

The culmination of the struggle was a hand-to-hand melee upon the steps of the Templo Mayor itself, as the remainder of the Eagle Warrior Society brothers fought to the death to defend Huitzilopotchli, their patron. In the process, every single temple in the city was desecrated, every altar was broken, and every statue was smashed. As the Spanish first looted and then consolidated their control over Tenochtitlan, they would finish this work by leaving behind few traces of the formal Aztec religion behind. In the years that followed, this pattern would be repeated over and over again throughout the lands ruled by Spain until all of the temples and pyramids would be eliminated.

Having subdued and destroyed Tenochtitlan, Cortés then attacked and destroyed the cities in the Valley of Mexico that had been allied with Aztecs. To top it all off, smallpox epidemics that were transferred to the natives from the Spanish wiped out an untold number even after the conquistadors left, with an estimated 10-50% of the remaining inhabitants killed. The numbers dwindled so much that the conquistadors actually merged smaller societies by forcibly transferring natives into larger population centers.

---

38 "Second Letter of Hernando Cortez to Charles V" full text available at the *Early Americas Digital Archive.* Accessed online at: http://mith.umd.edu/eada/html/display.php?docs=cortez_letter2.xml

Thus, in the span of just a few years, the Aztec empire was almost completely wiped out, and only a few decades after the arrival of Cortés' armies in 1519, the Aztec religion was shattered, the temples were destroyed, the pyramids had churches on top (or were obliterated, as was the case of the Templo Mayor), the priesthoods were killed or driven underground, and none of the grand public rituals took place.

The physical destruction of the temples would eliminate the places of worship and end the principal festivals and rituals (including the practice of human sacrifice), but it would not completely eliminate the religion itself. To do this, the Spanish sent out a second army consisting of Franciscans, Dominicans and Jesuits to set up missionary posts throughout Latin America, slowly but effectively converting the people to Catholicism. In its place, Roman Catholicism took deep roots in the landscape of Mesoamerica and is still the dominant faith of Mexico today.

When it came to "Christianizing" Quetzalcoatl, it was easier than usual to intertwine this indigenous god with Christian beliefs. Catholics like Father Diego de Duran, who wrote in the 16th century, took descriptions of Quetzalcoatl being bearded and of having a white face to mean that he was actually the living Christ who went out into the world to spread His message. That there is a story of Topiltzin-Quetzalcoatl being born of a virgin only served to fuel this leap of faith.

Indeed, there are similarities between some of the stories and those in the Bible. Diego de Duran explained one such coincidence when he asked for information about Quetzalcoatl's departure: "He began to relate to me the fourteenth chapter of Exodus, saying that Quetzalcoatl had arrived at the sea with many people and that he continued and had struck the sea with a staff and it had dried up and become a road through which he entered, both he and his people. Also that his persecutors had entered after him and the waters had returned to their place and nothing more was known of them."[39] That said, it's important to note that this was as much a retelling of an original myth as it was a local metamorphosis of the story in order to put it into a setting that was familiar to the Spanish. There is such evidence of local Mesoamericans reshaping their own lore to place it in a system which they had no choice but to accommodate.[40]

The association of Quetzalcoatl with Jesus Christ is an endeavor taken up heartily by the Church of Latter Day Saints as well. In a fairly extensive article in the *Journal of Book of Mormon Studies*, Diane E. Wirth claims that there are "plausible associations" between Christ and Quetzalcoatl, including "[being] a deity playing a role in the creation; associated with the bread of life (meaning 'maize' here); assisting the dead; shedding blood to save mankind; a deity dying on a tree; resurrecting and being responsible for the rebirth of the deceased; a personage of light who is associated with the sun."[41] Of course, this is still a somewhat tenuous list of

---

[39] Historia de las indias de Nueva España e islas de la tierra firme, 1:12
[40] See Gardner 1986

associations since there are few cultures in the world that do not have some deity or deities with the same similarities.

Discovering a real association with Jesus Christ was the hope of not just the Mormons but also Diego de Duran too. He desperately hoped and searched for a Gospel written in Hebrew that would prove Jesus or Saint Thomas, the "wandering saint," had visited the "New World." He did not find one, but he did find numerous indigenous screenfold manuscripts which he did not bother to preserve.[42]

An interesting aspect of the connection with Saint Thomas dates to 1794, when the Dominican priest Servando Teresa de Mier delivered a sermon in which he criticized the colonial officials for their corruption and claimed that the "glory of the conquest of Mexico" had nothing to do with the Spanish. According to de Mier, the conquest was actually foretold a thousand years beforehand when Saint Thomas appeared in Mexico and whose memory subsequently remained in the form of Quetzalcoatl.

Eventually, Quetzalcoatl became adopted by those in favor of independence, and he has been a symbol of Mexican individualism ever since. In the 20th century, Quetzalcoatl became a major symbol in the *indigenismo* movement, a political ideology present in many American countries that sought to raise the profile of indigenous peoples. Quetzalcoatl became a symbol of the Mexican people, and his role as a cultural hero was emphasized by many artists both in Mexico and abroad.

### Online Resources

Other books about Mesoamerica by Charles River Editors

Other books about Quetzalcoatl on Amazon

### Bibliography

Bernal, Díaz de Castillo (1632/1963) The Conquest of New Spain Penguin Classics

Bowie, F., (2007) The Anthropology of Religion, An Introduction Blackwell

Campbell, J. (2008) The Hero With A Thousand Faces University of Princeton Frazer,

Carrasco, D., (2012) The Aztec: A Very Short Introduction Oxford University Press

Garner, B., (1986) The Christianization of Quetzalcoatl: A History of the Metamorphosis Sunstone Magazine Issue 11: 6-10

---

[41] Wirth 2002
[42] Carrasco 2012

Hyde, L., (2008) Trickster Makes This World: How Disruptive Imagination Creates Culture Canongate Books

Jordan, D. K., Readings in Classical Nahuatl: The Death of Quetzalcoatl University of San Diego

Kirk, G. S., (1996) Myth: Its Meaning And Function In Ancient And Other Cultures California

Knight, A., (2012) Mexico From The Beginning To The Spanish Conquest Cambridge University Press

Miller, Mary; Karl Taube (1993). The Gods and Symbols of Ancient Mexico and the Maya. Thames and Hudson.

Read, K., (2000) Mesoamerican Mythology: A Guide To The Gods, Heroes, Rituals, And Beliefs Of Mexico And Central America Oxford University Press

Shara, R & Traxler, L (2005) The Ancient Maya Stanford University Press

Townsent, R., (2009) The Aztec Thames and Hudson

Wirth, D. E., (2002) Quetzalcoatl, the Maya Maize God, and Jesus Christ, Journal of Book of Mormon Studies 11/1

## Free Books by Charles River Editors

We have brand new titles available for free most days of the week. To see which of our titles are currently free, click on this link.

# Discounted Books by Charles River Editors

We have titles at a discount price of just 99 cents everyday. To see which of our titles are currently 99 cents, click on this link.

Printed in Great Britain
by Amazon

55151334R00032